Chicago, Chicago, that is the town for me
Chicago, Chicago, that is the town for me

Eurreal Wilford 'Little Brother'
Montgomery
(1906–1985)

"

Before there was a city of Chicago, Native Americans knew about a marshy area they called Chigagou, meaning 'the wild-garlic place.' To these American Indians, Chigago was an inhospitable place, and few wanted to live on the area's marshy land.

Robert Spinney
(b. 1961)

"

Chicago has been called the 'windy' city, the term being used metaphorically to make out that Chicagoans were braggarts. The city is losing this reputation, for the reason that as people got used to it they found most of her claims to be backed up by facts.

Freeborn County Standard
(20 November 1892)

In the late 1700s and early 1800s, daring Americans seeking the excitement and potential wealth of the frontier headed for the remote settlement of Chigagou. Upon arriving there, they found a typical North American frontier settlement: wealthy speculators, dirty fur trappers, and fugitives from justice all sought shelter in run-down flophouses… land was cheap. Alcohol was cheaper.

Robert Spinney
(b. 1961)

"

Here was a city which had no
tradition but was making them, and
this was the very thing that everyone
seemed to understand and rejoice in.
Chicago was like no other city in the
world, so said they all.

*Guide to the Columbian
World's Fair*
    (1892)

"

"

What more wonderful, more strange, more beyond belief, than the growth of Chicago's greatness.

A Strangers' and Tourists' Guide to the City of Chicago
(1866)

"

"

Chi-CA-go: An unchallenged murder record—a splendid university—hobo capital to the country—railroad ruler, corn baron, liquor king—and the finest of grand opera. Altogether the most zestful spectacle on this sphere.

Advertisement,
The Chicagoan
(1927)

"

This is Chicago, where mankind invented the skyscraper, Frank Lloyd Wright walked the streets, and a trip to the ballpark isn't supposed to feel like a drive to the shopping mall.

Chicago Tribune
(26 June 1991)

Nothing that either man or nature can do, apparently, can check the growth of this city that has spread back from the lake like a prairie fire... Young as she is, Chicago has become the pace-maker of the world.

Munsey's Magazine
(April 1907)

Catastrophes invite investigation. The sheer magnitude of destruction and loss of life raise the obvious question of causality: 'How did it happen?' When evidence is not conclusive, folk traditions arise, offering explanations that become embedded in popular culture. Such is the case with the 1871 Great Chicago Fire, Mrs O'Leary, and her cow.

Chicago Tribune
(21 February 1983)

> I saw a man, he danced with his wife
> He had the time, the time of his life
> In Chicago, Chicago, my home town!

Fred Fisher
(1875–1942)

66

The greater the risk, the more harsh the adversity, and the more substantial the challenge, the more durable Chicagoans became.

Perry R. Duis
(b. 1943)

99

In the midst of a calamity without parallel in the world's history, looking upon the ashes of thirty years' accumulations, the people of this once beautiful city have resolved that CHICAGO SHALL RISE AGAIN!

Chicago Tribune
(9 October 1871, the day after the Great Fire)

I tell you, within five years Chicago's business houses will be rebuilt, and by the year 1900 the new Chicago will boast a population of a million souls… she has only to wait a few short years for the sure development of her manifest destiny!

Chicago Tribune
(9 October 1871, the day after the Great Fire)

Even when Chicago was a raw, jerry-built, lawless, amoral, cholera-ridden town, Chicagoans had greedy faith in it and didn't want to go back to wherever they'd come from or push on farther west.

Chicago: An Extraordinary Guide
(1968)

"

Let me tell you something. I'm from Chicago. I don't break.

Barack Obama, quoted in the *Chicago Tribune* (24 July 2009)

"

> As soon as a Chicago artist won his spurs, he packed his paint kit and took a fast train to New York.

Walter Sherwood
(1871–1965)

66

In 1890, Chicago boasted a population of 1,099,850… between 1830 and 1890, Chicago was the fastest-growing city on the globe. Its population expanded almost 37 times during those 60 years, and its borders expanded rapidly as well.

Greg Borzo
(b. 1954)

99

" "

In 1889 Chicago had the peculiar
qualifications of growth which made...
adventuresome pilgrimages even on the
part of young girls plausible. Its many
and growing commercial opportunities
gave it widespread fame, which made of it
a giant magnet, drawing to itself, from all
quarters, the hopeful and the hopeless.

Theodore Dreiser
(1871–1945)

" "

"

City of immigrants or city of heartless plutocrats, say what you will, Chicago almost defies interpretation. In many ways Chicago is like a snake that sheds its skin every thirty years or so and puts on a new coat to conform to a new reality.

Dominic Pacyga
(b. 1949)

"

The depression that began in 1930 and was ended ten years later only by a massive program of military procurement was a disaster for the nation as a whole but an absolute and unmitigated calamity for Chicago... the Sophoclean reversal of fortune, from the expansive forces of the twenties that seemed to have no limit to the impotence and hopelessness of the thirties.

Carl W. Condit
(1914–1997)

"

I give you Chicago. It is not London-and-Harvard. It is not Paris-and-buttermilk. It is American in every chitling and sparerib, and it is alive from snout to tail.

H.L. Mencken
Chicago Tribune
(28 October 1917)

"

66

Perhaps the most typically American
place in America.

James Bryce
(1838–1922)

99

The most civilized city in America? Chicago, of course! In Chicago there is the mysterious something …

H.L. Mencken
Chicago Tribune
(28 October 1917)

"

To visit Chicago is like entering
a new world.

*A Strangers' and Tourists' Guide
to the City of Chicago*
(1866)

"

"

I adore Chicago. It is the pulse
of America.

Sarah Bernhardt
(1844–1923)

"

"

The simplicity of life in Chicago is considered its greatest charm. Men drift into the clubs, dine, go to the theatre, drop into a whist party, or go to supper in the same clothes that they put on when they start to business in the same morning.

St James's Gazette
      (6 September 1888)

"

" This is a great uninteresting place of 600,000 inhabitants.

Matthew Arnold
(1822–1888)
"

I fancy the place I have been in that was most like Greece was a gathering of university scholars in Chicago! The city was disorderly but very much alive.

Junius Lucien Price
(1883–1964)

66

Come and show me another city with
lifted head singing so proud to be alive
and coarse and strong and cunning.

Poetry Magazine
(March 1914)

99

The men or women who can not amuse themselves in Chicago must be confirmed misanthropes, finding no joy in life anywhere.

Rand, McNally & Co's Handy Guide to Chicago
(1892)

"

If Chicago is to be the Capital of
Civilization, it is indispensable that
she should at least be able to show
that every resident within her limits
enjoyed every advantage which
intelligent and public-spirited
administration has secured for
people elsewhere.

William T. Stead
(1849–1912)

"

66

We are known as 'the city that works.'
You gotta make sure it works for
everybody and not just a few.

Rahm Emanuel
(b. 1959)

99

"

I assert that writers associated with Chicago transformed American literary standards by representing the diverse and changing accents of modern urban life.

Lisa Woolley

"

To the professional mediocrity, therefore, Chicago is today a city of golden opportunity... But to the writer seeking to work creatively, it is a kick in the palatinate.

Nelson Algren
(1909–1981)

With its customary audacity, the city built [the 1893 World's Columbian Exposition] on an apparently impossible sandy site along the lakefront eight miles south of the river, and it drew over 27,000,000 people.

Irving Cutler
(b. 1923)

66

Chicago has often been described as
'a city of neighborhoods', a phrase
that encapsulates both its strengths
and weaknesses. Chicago's numerous
ethnic neighborhoods provide
stimulating, diverse environments;
Chicago has also been called the
most segregated city in America.

Lynne Warren
(b. 1952)

99

"

Chicago has a temperament ideally suited to tom-tom beating and fireworks and hurrah showmanship. It bursts to the buttons with a civic pride... It is as self-conscious as a Saturday afternoon window-dresser, as naïve as a schoolboy's conception of George Washington, as noisy as an evangelist.

Architectural Forum
(1934)

"

"

[In Richard J. Daley's time] the neighborhood-towns were part of larger ethnic states. To the north of the Loop was Germany. To the northwest was Poland. To the west were Italy and Israel. To the southwest were Bohemia and Lithuania. And to the south was Ireland... you could always tell, even with your eyes closed, which state you were in by the odors of the food stores and the open kitchen windows.

Mike Royko
(1932–1997)

"

From the beginning, breweries [in Chicago] had often demonstrated an ethnic secularism typical of Chicago neighborhoods. Almost every early immigrant group had its own churches, schools, and brewery.

Bob Skilnik
(b. 1950)

66

It's impossible to root for the White Sox and the Cubs at the same time. Like being a Republican AND a Democrat, that's just not how it works. You must choose.

Nico Lang

99

If there is any justice in the world, to be a Sox fan frees a man from any other form of penance.

William Veeck
(1914–1986)

Every Chicago baseball fan owns
a controlling interest in the Cubs—
in his own mind.

William Wrigley Jr.
(1861–1932)

"

I love Chicago, but I didn't think I had enough soul to be a Cubs fan.

Mary Buckheit

"

In most places in the country, voting is looked upon as a right and a duty, but in Chicago it's a sport. In Chicago not only your vote counts, but all kinds of other votes – kids, dead folks, and so on.

Dick Gregory
(b. 1932)

The 'L' is under tremendous financial strain, but just one 'L' train can keep hundreds of automobiles off the street, and that means a lot in this era of rising gasoline prices and concerns about global warming.

Greg Borzo
(b. 1954)

I have given up on the lakeshore.
It is becoming a Chicago version of
Rio de Janiero's Copacabana – a solid
row of high-rises with Appalachia
directly behind.

Harry Weese
(1915–1998)

"

The founders and the cast of the Second City… were university people, imbued with respect for intellectualism and the great masterworks. We had all served our apprenticeship in the classical theater. We never thought of ourselves as popular entertainers.

Bernie Sahlins
(1922–2013)

"

The infamous 'Second City syndrome'
that has plagued all areas of Chicago life
has nowhere had such a deleterious
effect as in the visual arts... a city that
has led the world in so many areas –
architecture, sociology, journalism,
transportation, manufacturing, and
more recently, sports and
improvisational theater and comedy –
may understandably fail to pay
attention to other arenas.

Kevin E. Consey

There is only one Frye Street. It runs
from the river to Grand Avenue where
the El is. All the World is there. It runs
from the safe solidity of honorable
marriage to all of the amazing varieties
of harlotry – from replicas of Old
World living to the obscenities of latter
decadence – from Heaven to Hell.
All the World is there.

Marita Bonner
(1899–1971)

We are proud of Milwaukee because she is not overrun with a lazy police force as is Chicago – because her morals are better, [the] criminals fewer, her credit better; and her taxes lighter in proportion to her valuation than Chicago, the windy city of the West.

Milwaukee Daily Sentinel
(4 July 1860)

"

People in Chicago, as a rule, haven't as much time to be wicked as the people of other cities.

The Lakeside Monthly
(1873)

"

Chicago's role in aviation changed over the years, often very rapidly… for many of the same geographic reasons that the city had become a maritime and railroad hub earlier, it now became the principal midcontinental aviation nexus… Municipal/Midway and O'Hare airport successively became the busiest in the world in terms of the volume of aircraft and passengers.

David Young
(b. 1940)

For Wright, Chicago represented the architectural 'Promised Land,' the land of milk and honey... As well as being a boom town, it was a progressive urban center where many new ideas were tested in architecture by new thinking on the part of the clients as well as the architects. Chicago is the location for nearly one quarter of Wright's existing buildings.

Thomas A. Heinz

"

We no longer send our architects
to Paris or Rome. Now Europeans
come to America, and specifically
to Chicago.

Hugh Dalziel Duncan
(1909–1970)

"

The public recreational space and the public institutions that Chicago established in the two decades following the adoption of the Burnham Plan represent the greatest and most valuable civic achievement of any American city.

Carl W. Condit
(1914–1997)

"

[In the 1920s] Jazz in Chicago gave
particularly sharp and memorable
musical expression to feelings of
giddy excitement and rebellious
daring, stimulating powerful
emotional experiences which
permanently shaped our collective
memory of that time and place.

William Howland Kenney
(b. 1940)

"

Four decades and more later, the blues of postwar Chicago remain the standard bearers, the yardstick by which all others have been and continue to be measured. [Muddy] Waters, his cohorts and immediate followers had limned definitively the contours of the style, and it was they who extended and reworked the idiom, bringing it to its highest levels.

Pete Welding
(1935–1995)

"

See, Chicago was known to be the mother of the blues for years and still is. Every good musician who ever left the South, he stopped in Chicago.

Otis Spann
(1930–1970)

"

66

Chicago during the soul [music] era easily ranked as one of the major centers for the production of soul and equalled or surpassed other regional centers in putting records on the charts.

Robert Pruter
(b. 1944)

99

Chicago is famous for many things, but the Well-Dressed Man is not one of them. However, even if we do not know how to dress, we should be immensely grateful that our ladies do.

Gene Markey
(1895–1980)

"

Most Chicago ethics came from
traditions which preferred to leave
decisions about the use of fleshly
pleasures to the Church and the
individual conscience, and which
permitted alcoholic beverages, Sunday
recreation, and the mother tongue.

John D. Buenker
(b. 1937)

"

If Christ came to Chicago he would find that many of the citizens have forgotten the existence of any moral law.

William T. Stead
(1849–1912)

"

Chicago has so much excellent
architecture that they feel obliged to
tear some of it down now and then and
erect terrible buildings just to help us all
appreciate the good stuff.

Audrey Niffenegger
(b. 1963)

"

Chicagoans like having a rich mayor; it gives them one less thing to worry about.

Jonathan Alter
(b. 1957)

"

Chicago is unique. It is the only
completely corrupt city in America.

Charles Merriam
(1874–1953)

"

"

I have heard that the Chicago girls are miserable flirts; but the remark always came from a woman whose flirting days were over, or from a man who could not hold his own at that sort of thing.

The Lakeside Monthly
(1873)

"

"

A city of terror and light, untamed.

W.L. George
(1882–1926)

"

It's one of the most progressive cities in the world. Shooting is only a sideline.

Will Rogers
(1879–1935)

66

I would not want to live there for anything in the world, but I think that whoever ignores it is not entirely acquainted with our century and of what it is the ultimate expression.

Giuseppe Giacosa
(1847–1906)

99

Hog butcher for the World,
Tool Maker, Stacker of Wheat,
Player with Railroads and the Nation's
Freight Handler;
Stormy, husky, brawling,
City of the Big Shoulders.

Carl Sandburg
(1878–1967)

"

Chicago, a term said to have denoted a king or deity, a skunk or a wild onion…

E.J. Goodspeed
(1833–1881)

"

The Wrigley Building, Chicago is
The Union Stockyard, Chicago is
One town that won't let you down
It's my kind of town!

Sammy Cahn
(1913–1993)

"

We are a multi-ethnic, multi-racial,
multi-language city and that is not a
source to negate but really a source of
pride, because it adds stability and
strength to a metropolitan city as
large as ours.

Harold Washington
(1922–1987)

"

"

Lucy carried in her mind a very individual map of Chicago: a blur of smoke and wind and noise, with flashes of blue water, and certain clear outlines rising from the confusion... This city of feeling rose out of the city of fact like a definite composition–beautiful because the rest was blotted out.

Willa Cather
(1873–1947)

"

66

Chicago is the product of modern
capitalism, and, like all other great
commercial centers, is unfit for
human habitation. The Illinois
Central Railroad Company selected
the site upon which the city is
built...a vast miasmatic swamp far
better suited to mosquito culture
than for human beings.

Eugene V. Debs
(1855–1926)

99

Chicago, queen and guttersnipe of cities, cynosure and cesspool of the world! ... the most beautiful and the most squalid, girdled with a twofold zone of parks and slums; where the keen air from lake and prairie is ever in the nostrils and the stench of foul smoke is never out of the throat.

George W. Steevens
(1869–1900)

66

Chicago ain't ready for reform yet!

Mathias 'Paddy' Bauler
(1890–1977)

99

"

I am going to St Petersburg, Florida, tomorrow. Let the worthy citizens of Chicago get their liquor the best they can. I'm sick of the job—it's a thankless one and full of grief. I've been spending the best years of my life as a public benefactor.

Alphonse Gabriel 'Al' Capone (1899–1947)

"

Chicago is America's dream, writ large and flamboyantly. It has—as they used to whisper of the town's fast women—a reputation.

Studs Terkel
(1912–2008)

66

City of the big shoulders was how the white-haired poet put it. Maybe meaning that the shoulders had to get that wide because they had so many bone-deep grudges to settle.

Nelson Algren
(1909–1981)

99

I had been so obsessed with consumer issues that I never noticed the plights of the city's neighborhoods. I saw despair in the faces of senior citizens, forgotten and lonely. Many expressed fear of the gangs that roamed the streets, grabbing their purses or their social security checks. Was this the Chicago that I loved? Yes, and it was part of Chicago I wanted to change.

Jane Byrne
(1933–2014)

It makes no difference that many of the old buildings have died, that many of the gangsters have died, that jazz has since moved to New York, or that the Chicago for which many search is so elusive. Visitors and residents alike pursue the legend that is CHICAGO.

Kenny J. Williams
(1927–2003)

Having seen [Chicago], I urgently desire never to see it again. It is inhabited by savages.

Rudyard Kipling
(1865–1936)

"

I no longer make my home in Chicago, but Chicago still makes its home in me. I have Chicago stories I have yet to write. So long as those stories kick inside me, Chicago will still be home.

Sandra Cisneros
(b. 1954)

"

One striking thing about Chicago is the number of idlers... [but] in every direction are the typical men of the town – pushing, surging, rushing, and working.

St James's Gazette
6 September 1888

Eventually, I think that Chicago will be the most beautiful great city left in the modern world.

Frank Lloyd Wright
(1867–1959)

Credits

The publisher gratefully thanks the many copyright holders below who have generously granted permission for the use of the quotations in this book. Every effort has been made to credit copyright holders of the quotations used in this book. We apologize for any unintentional omissions or errors and will insert the appropriate acknowledgement to any companies or individuals in the subsequent editions of the book.

p.1, Eurreal Wilford 'Little Brother' Montgomery, *Lake Front Blues* (1935); p.2, Robert Spinney, *City of Big Shoulders: A History of Chicago* (2000); p.3, *Freeborn County Standard*, Albert Lea, MN, 20 November, 1892; p.4, Robert Spinney, *City of Big Shoulders: A History of Chicago* (2000), p. 13; p.5, *Guide to the Columbian World's Fair, 1892*; *Strangers' and Tourists Guide to the City of Chicago* (1866), p. 20; p.7, Advertisement, *The Chicagoan*, 1927; p.8, *Chicago Tribune*, 26 June 1991; p.9, *Munsey's Magazine*, April 1907; p.10, *Chicago Tribune*, 21 February 1983; p.11, Fred Fisher, *Chicago ('That Toddlin' Town)* (1922); p.12, Perry R. Duis, *Challenging Chicago: Coping With Daily Life, 1837–1920* (2007) , p. 358; p.13, *Chicago Tribune*, 9 October 1871; p.14, *Chicago Tribune*, 9 October 1871; p.15, Jory Graham, *Chicago: An Extraordinary Guide*, Chicago, (1967), p. xi; p.16, Barack Obama, *Chicago Tribune*, 24 July 2009; p.17, Walter Sherwood, *Chicago: The World's Youngest Great City* (1929), p. 35; p.18, Greg Borzo, *The Chicago "L"* (2007), p. 11; p.19, Theodore Dreiser, *Sister Carrie*, Bantam Books, (1900), p. 19; p.20, Dominic Pacyga, *Chicago: A Biography*, (2009), p. 1; p.21, Carl W. Condit, *Chicago 1930–70: Building, Planning and Urban Technology* (1974), p. 3; p.22, H.L. Mencken, 'Civilized Chicago', in *Chicago Tribune*, 28 October 1917; p.23, James Bryce, *The American Commonwealth* (1888); p.24, H.L.

Mencken, 'Civilized Chicago', in *Chicago Tribune*, 28 October 1917;
p.25, *A Strangers' and Tourists' Guide to the City of Chicago* (1866), p.
20; p.26, Sarah Bernhardt, n.r.; p.27, *St James's Gazette*, 6 September
1888; p.28, Matthew Arnold, letter to his sister, 23 January 1884;
p.29, Lucien Price, *Dialogues of Alfred North Whitehead* (1954), p.
56; p.30, Carl Sandburg, 'Chicago', in *Poetry Magazine*, March 1914;
p.31, *Rand, McNally & Co's Handy Guide to Chicago* (1892), p. 57; p.
32, William T. Stead, *If Christ Came to Chicago* (1894), p. 326; p. 33,
Rahm Emanuel, 'Meet the New Boss', in *The Atlantic Monthly*
online, 27 February 2012; p.34, Lisa Woolley, *American Voices of the
Chicago Renaissance* (2000), p. ix; p.35, Nelson Algren, *Chicago: City
on the Make*, afterword to 2nd edn., (1961), p. 89; p.36, Irving Cutler,
Chicago: Metropolis of the Mid-Continent (1976), p. 33; p.37, Lynne
Warren, *Art in Chicago, 1945–95* (1996), p. 83; p.38, 'A Century of
Progress Paradox', in *Architectural Forum*, LXI, November 1934, p.
374; p.39, Mikey Royko, *Boss: Richard J. Daley of Chicago* (1971), pp.
30–31; p.40, Bob Skilnik, *The History of Beer and Brewing in
Chicago, 1833–1978* (1999), p. vii–viii; p.42, William Veeck, *Veeck—
as in Wreck: The Autobiography of Bill Veeck* (1962), p. 336; p.43, Julie
Fenster, *In the Words of Great Business Leaders*, (1999), p. 35; p.44,
Mary Buckheit, 'Like Baseball, Emmylou Harris is Back', ESPN.
com, April 21, 2011 http://sports.espn.go.com/espn/thelife/music/
news/story?id=6386196); p.45, Dick Gregory, *Dick Gregory's
Political Primer* (1972), p. 69; p.47, Bernie Sahlins, *Days and Nights
at the Second City* (2001), p. 11; p.49, Kevin Consey, *Art in Chicago,
1945–9* (1996), p. 8; p.50, Maria Bonner, *Frye Street and Environs: The
Collected Works of Marita Bonner (ca. 1930)* (1987); p. 51, *Milwaukee
Daily Sentinel*, 4 July 1860, p. 1; p.52, Francis Fisher Browne, *The
Lakeside Monthly*, vol. 10 (October 1873), p.329; p.53, David Young,
Chicago Aviation: An Illustrated History (2003), p. viii; p.54, Thomas
A. Heinz, *Frank Lloyd Wright Field Guide, Metrochicago Volume 2*
(1997), p. 10; p.55, Hugh Dalziel Duncan, *Culture and Democracy:
The Struggle for Form in Society and Architecture in Chicago and the
Middle West during the Life and Times of Louis H. Sullivan* (1965), p.

xxi; p.56, Carl W. Condit, *Chicago 1930–70: Building, Planning and Urban Technology* (1974), p. 3; p.57 William Howland Kenney, *Chicago Jazz: A Cultural History, 1904–1930* (1993), p. xiv; p.58 Pete Welding, 'Gone to Mainstreet', in *Bluesland* (1992); p.59, Otis Spann, 'The Blues, Chicago Style', in *Chicago History*, Spring-Summer 1974, p. 10; p.60, Robert Putter, *Chicago Soul* (1991), p. xiv; p.61 Gene Makrey, *The Chicagoan*, 24 September 1927; p.62, William T. Stead, *If Christ Came to Chicago* (1894), p. 326; p.64, Audrey Niffenegger, *The Time Traveler's Wife* (2003), p. 339; p. 65, Jonathan Alter, 'Meet the New Boss', in *The Atlantic Monthly* online, 27 February 2012; p.66, Charles Merriam in discussion with A. J. Liebling, 1911; p.67, Francis Fisher Browne, *The Lakeside Monthly*, vol. 10 (October 1873), p.331; p. 68, W.L. George, *Hail Columbia!* (1921), 37; p.69, Will Rogers, Stephen Colbert, *The Colbert Report*, on *Comedy Central*, 3 September 2013; p.70, Guiseppe Giacosa, *As Others See Chicago*, ed. by Bessie Louise Pierce (1933), p. 267; p. 71, Carl Sandberg, Chicago', in *Poetry Magazine*, March 1914, p.191; p. 72, E.J. Goodspeed, *History of the Great Fires in Chicago and the West* (1871), p. 19; p. 73, Sammy Cahn, *My Kind of Town*, lyrics Sammy Cahn, music Jimmy Van Heusen (1964); p.74, Harol Washington, inaugural speech, 29 April, 1983; p.75, Will Cather, *Lucy Gayheart* (1935), p. 20; p. 76, Eugene V. Debs, *Chicago Socialist*, 25 October 1902, pp. 319–20; p.77, George W. Steevens, *The Land of the Dollar* (1897), p. 144; p.78, Mathias 'Paddy' Bauler, *The Mayors: The Chicago Political Tradition*, 4th edn. (2013), p. 145; p.79, Alphonese Gabriel Capone, *Chicago Tribune*, 1 December 1927, p. 1; p.80, Studs Terkel, *Studs Terkel's Chicago* (1996), p. 12; p.81, Nelson Algren, *Chicago: City on the Make* (1951), p. 62; p.82, Jane Byrne, *My Chicago* (1992), p. 267; p.83, Kenny J. Williams, *In the City of Men* (1974), p. 5; p.84, Rudyard Kipling, *From Sea to Sea* (1920); p.85, Sandra Cisneros, *The House on Mango Street* (2009), p. xxiv; p.86, *St James's Gazette*, 6 September 1888; p.87, Frank Lloyd Wright, London lecture, 1939, in *The Future of Architecture*, Horizon Press, 1953, p. 260.